As Orion Falls

AS

ORION

FALLS

aaron a. abeyta

GRp

Ghost Road Press
Denver, Colorado

Library of Congress Cataloging-in-Publication Data.
Abeyta, Aaron A. (1971 —).
As Orion Falls.
Ghost Road Press
ISBN 0-9760729-7-1 (pbk.)
Library of Congress Control Number: 2005927701

The following poems have originally appeared in these publications:
"as orion falls," "for the unidentified mexican national who died at 5:00 p.m. somewhere between san luis and manassa his van rolling 3¼ times" and "love poem after a passing antelope" in *Pilgrimage.* "definition," "love poem after a passing antelope," and "elegy on spring and other losses" in *A*, the Colorado State University Literary Review.

Book Design: Sonya Unrein
Cover Painting: Marvin Muniz

Ghost Road Press
Denver, Colorado
ghostroadpress.com

acknowledgments

i have come to believe that there is much beauty in the world, that amongst the pillars of hardship and the foundations of pain there is a shelter of goodness and beauty. this was a difficult realization, one that took years. finally, i understand that there are many heavy things placed in our scale, this balancing we know as life. often the scale seems staggeringly tilted toward the side of us that carries pain, but i know now that a small weight of love, of understanding, and of faith is capable of bringing balance. therefore, i am thankful to the many who brought this trinity of healing back into my poems, my life, and my view of the world.

most notable in this process of healing, this book, these poems, was my beautiful and powerful wife Michele who has taught me the many nuances of love and of strength. for her i am always grateful. even if there were no such thing as poetry, i imagine i would create it to describe her, to contain her, to represent what is in the deepest roots of her being, strength, beauty and love. for Michele i am thankful, eternally.

i would also like to thank my mother and father, Martha and Alfonzo, amazing people who personify integrity and perseverance. from them i have learned how to stand again, the ability to always rise from adversity. they have also given me a great appreciation for and knowledge of what is just, fair and meaningful, making sure that these things are never compromised and always worth standing up for, even if, at times, we must stand alone. to them, also eternally, i am thankful.

muchas gracias to all of my abuelitas and abuelitos and their beautiful gift of family and culture. also, thanks to all of my tias y tios for their support.

for the other members of my family, brothers Al and Andrew and my sister Anycia and their spouses, Lisa, Lori and Hal. Thank you, all of you, for your support, for your older sibling examples of how to be: Anycia, for her amazing generosity, beauty, strength and for her example of hard work and the importance of education, Andrew, for his strength, hard work, knowledge of beauty, and for keeping my abuelito's customs and traditions alive, Al, my oldest brother who has taught me patience, humor and unwavering ethics, he too is generous and strong and i thank him along with the others.

also, thank you to my beautiful nieces and nephews: Chelsea, A.J., Brittny, Adam, Jasmine, Austin and Miquela; Justin and Ashlyn; Rianna, Clorinda, Andrew, Amber, and Amos; and Andres Javier.

many thanks to the other members of my family, especially the Trujillos, Michele's amazing and talented family, Mike, Alice, Miguel, Andie, Ana, and Marcel. each of them is an integral part of mine and Michele's life. thank you, each of you, for always supporting us and for the many blessings of your presence.

also, many thanks to my friends and supporters: namely Bill Tremblay (Guillermo), my mentor, my friend, the person who taught me how to love a single word, my poet friend whose voice often guides my own poetry; Carol, my dear friend, fellow poet and confidant who is always willing to share poetry, for her guidance and unwavering friendship i am grateful; Renee, my lifelong friend and beautiful person, i miss your voice echoing down the halls, but d.c. will benefit from your enthusiasm and great spirit; Alex and Bonnie, my dear friends who have always supported my work and have done much to make me understand the layers of strength and understanding that can be found in literature; to Juan Felipe Herrera, a brilliant writer and example of the human spirit who i am honored to call a friend; many thanks to George Sibley and Karen Wuest, both of you inspire me and i thank you for that, there are poems in here which you shared in the creation of.

Mark and Wayne, thanks to the two of you for always sharing your work and being generous with your edits and critiques of mine; Sue Ellen and John for always pointing me toward outlets for my work, both of you are generous and good people; Deanna Ludwin for her omnipresent smile and support; and many thanks to Stella and Brittny, who both helped with early drafts of this book.

i would also like to thank Father Felix and Father Pat, both of whom laid an important foundation for healing and understanding. of course i would be remiss if i did not also thank God for abundant blessings and for the stones of pain and hardship he laid in my path. without those stones one might never know the capacity a person has for love and forgiveness, both of which are equal parts of beauty.

for angels
therefore
Michele

Contents

definition

where does the poem come from
some think it is God
others suffering
i believed at some point
that poem and place were the same
a map of the washboard
roads of someone's existence
then there are those
pulling poems from
the air into their nets

i think of Pablo
he would probably say
the poem is the spaces
between the mesh net

not what we bring to our hands
or ashore but
what escapes us
the water flowing
back to her mother
the butterfly pushed away
by the whoosh of the net

poems are like people
they come from everywhere

still there is no definition
that is mine
no meteorite burning red
in the 3:00 a.m. sky
no brief electricity
of a first kiss
define define define
the poem is
what would have happened
if Tristan and Isolde had lived
some mad potion
that is supposed to be death
and is instead
the way we fall and live
more fully because we have fallen

po-em *n* 1: a word that is the name of something. 2: the moment when
the word becomes something. i.e. as in the moment when we should be
sleeping but wait up in case she has one more beautiful thing to say.

po·em *v* 1: a word that expresses an act, occurrence, or mode of being. 2: to build freely. i.e. a roof made of words or a wall constructed of silence.

po·em *prep* 1: *pre* + *ponere*, to put. 2: a form that combines with a noun or pronoun that has a relation to some other word. i.e. to be *at* a state of revision or to be *on* the cusp of some unthought thought.

po·em *adj* 1: often formed by adding endings such as -able, -ful and -ish to nouns or verbs. 2: relating to or functioning as beautiful, clear or something like sunlight on a first snow.

po·em *adv* 1: form by adding -ly to an adjective, thus making it even more poetic, exceptions are lovely, brotherly, friendly. add freely to amazing, brilliant or beautiful or any force of nature requiring one more syllable to be remembered. i.e. the sunrise that february morning was burning brilliantly for all the souls that would leave that day.

po·em *conj* 1: the act of conjoining, or the occurrence together in time or space. 2: linguistic form that joins together sentences, clauses, phrases, words, or time and space. i.e. a red bird flying into a cloud or squinting one's eyes at night to make all the stars one light.

po·em *interj* 1: word immediately following a poem. 2: word that moves you to a better or more introspective place. i.e. wow, yes, and oh my.

and then there is still
this lack of my own definition
and where it will persist
the backbeat of a song
that is its heart
the things we wish to say
and don't
the way unsaid things
try to live
even as we kill them
here is my definition
tomorrow there will be
a new river
but today at 10:03 a.m.
on a friday
the poem is thursday and saturday
it is what burns us
makes us love
what used to be
as we hope that
tomorrow the poem will be
newborn again into the sky
much like venus or our sun
in the hours before we wake.

a true love poem

i meet him at dusk
in the field with the old
broken wagon
an ice hauler
from a river now
thinly frozen

this wagon
wheels missing
floor boards of missing teeth
my abuelito's
simple memory
of Orlando and his leaving
do you remember how he cried when he had to go

from here i can see
la otra vanda
the river stripped sticks used
to leap over fences
the herd Orlando and my father followed
how it ended in autumn
and how one of the boys cried

my abuelito
says that sometimes
he feels like his old wagon
the loads the two of them
must have carried
their weight of ice
summers that melted around them

here is your true love poem
it is an old man's words
from a wheelchair
the way his eyes
filled with thin tears
that did not fall
the way he
remembered Orlando
and only this boy heard

omission
for Beatrice

dear abuelita
i have not forgotten you
in the poems people say
are for the common people
how can i say it
you are here
though there is no page
with your image on it
your seat at the table is empty
and these days
we bring the sick lambs
into our own homes
and place them on old shirts
in front of the fireplace

i am not exaggerating
everything that grows loved you
your hands with their crooked fingers
took in what no one loved or noticed
those sparrows i killed
their mud nests broken among
the small pale eggs
some part of you could not forgive me
though you let me go
with only a stiff finger to the chest

no one collects palitos
in a tin bucket
though i think you should know
i used to
and yes the fire would light every time

i still love bread
think of you on fridays
and wish somehow that there was not
this thing of age
where calendars let no one escape
i wish for that bus ride
where i would get off

at the gate to your house
the scent of bread filling the yard
the wild cats that loved only you
resting on the red roof

somehow i don't know the origin
but i think of you standing
at a screen door
your penco lambs waiting
for their milk which you would
always mix into clean bottles
i've said it once before
you loved completely
what no one else wanted

your pantry shelves
full of empty bottles and coffee cans
how can i say it
it took over twenty years
for me to understand
that those sparrows
were only eating the chokecherries
high on the tree
that we could not reach
and these many years later
i finally understand
why the lambs you could not save
dying in front of the wood stove
would begin moving their legs
as if they were running
even though death had already
left their mouths cold
perhaps it is naive or too pretty to think this
but i know they were running
through a meadow
they would never see on earth
but know nonetheless
before the earth thawed

why do the lambs
begin their running just before
and why do our eyes
give us away just before
and why would someone like you
with hands that bread loved
have to stop eating just before

there is no point to it
i know from what you taught me
that even things that grow
can be loved too late
or not enough
please do not think that of me
my omission
i still remember
the scent of baking bread
and see you as if
through a screen door
your warm house filling
with forgotten things

Ramon Fernandez—his trials, moments of light and happiness

Ramon Fernandez
lived a very symbolic life
and had spent his entire life
trying to become
himself

his father worked too hard
had hands which were
never known to be soft
his father understood things
which Ramon
would never grasp

the story
he had always loved her
Ramon knew this
by the way his hand shook
the way his thumb fit
perfectly on the ball of her foot
he loved her so much
he made promises

a house
children
a good stove
a wood pile which would never diminish
shoes which would last for years
love

he promised all he could
then promised more
goat's milk
to plant more beans than any man alive
a horse she could name
Ramon Fernandez lived a very symbolic life
she picked the name west

the romance
Ramon brushed beside her once
he imagined the smell of her hair
spring wheat
the freshest colors smells and desires
were mixed imagined and re-imagined
in his thought he loved her

Ramon only wanted
one moment
his thoughts of her
led him to a river
where they would skip rocks
during the year's first snowfall

here he would show her
the nature of stone
define the smooth dimensions
necessary to
glide across water
her whisper

he would explain
the need to be
parallel with the water
the one motion needed
to set stone
in flight

the water was beautiful
the way
it reproduced its feelings
without thought
in a manner more consistent
than the world's greatest loves

for Ramon knew
if he could bring her here
to this water
this first snow
she would love him
consistently without thought

the snow would melt
on their foreheads
noses
palms
knees
every stone wet
with what had to be love

the rain
Ramon Fernandez prayed daily
he prayed that the rain would not come
so that his lambs would grow
and he prayed that the rains would come
so that the grass would grow
he prayed and prayed and never really knew
for what he prayed
Ramon had spent his entire life waking
to the dissipation of clouds
which he would then watch regather themselves
above the western mountains
as a boy he thought every mountain
was named sangre de cristo
it was later that he learned that some mountains
are named after saints
he had heard once that the roads out here
were not marked with any sign
but he had seen a sign once
rocks smooth and wet which spelled out
dios es amor
this was his first sign
and from that day forward he knew
the roads were marked
the marks not always visible yet he knew they
were blood

Ramon's life was as symbolic as the rain
and so it came one day that Ramon Fernandez
fell trying to outrun the rain
he had prayed that morning for the soul
of his brother
for the fields of his dead uncle
and he prayed that it wouldn't rain
because he had carried his love
so long and it was finally spring

Ramon prayed again that afternoon
he prayed that his horse would not bleed to death
Ramon had run his horse so hard
he wanted to outrun the rain
to arrive at his love's door
his boots shining like a horse's back
beneath the spring sun
as he stood there the blood flowing onto his hands
he knew that all was lost

the stick had come up quick
the horse's hoof sending it upward
into her own belly where the unborn colt
named west was beginning to grow his mane
Ramon had made promises
none of which were keepable
so he prayed that his love and his horse would live
but he was alone and the
rain had finally begun to fall

dead horses
Ramon's father
had told him once
that the world
was a dying horse
easy to ride
hard to catch

Ramon burned his dead horse
and the unborn colt
named west
he could not bear
for the horse to remain motionless
he found smoke more fitting
it was something he would know
his entire life
Ramon Fernandez
took the blood soaked stick with him
he was never again seen without it
the stick which had killed
the last living horse
the link between Ramon and his love

there were other horses
which Ramon would not ride
his father's horse
ridden too much
a horse whose back did not shine
the world was dead horses
he prayed that they would rest
that he would no longer hear
their hooves in the light just before dark
trying to outrun the rain
Ramon Fernandez
wrote letters to his love
explaining that a man
without horses
was not a man to make promises
'dear love
i will spend my life alone
following these sheep
these sheep which i will call
betrayals'

in the end
as Ramon sat back
years later
he could swear he heard something
he pondered the voices   their music
the rustling of the sheep
he considered every sound
he had ever known
this was still not the sound he heard
the sound
he thought
must be the passing of his dreams
his love riding by
on his dead horse
but the sound was none of these things
it was simply the land moving
although he rejected it
he knew the sound was true
that it would follow him
like the rain

87ᵗʰ birthday

so here is how i will remember this place, my father arm wrestling with
his 87 year old father. "let him win" someone says quietly, so that my
abuelito will not hear. "viejo pero no espuelaio" he declares when he beats
my father. my abuelito defines this place, small house with thick adobe
walls where my grandmother kept wild cats fed, almost loved.
from the kitchen window you can see the mogotes, blue at dusk, just
before dark. at this window my abuelo would shave in the early mornings
in almost this same light, slightly more orange and much quieter as he
had the kitchen to himself. he is 87 now, and in his memory he claims to
have seen the conejos river from that window. now there are trees, green
in summer, which twist along the vega marking the river's path. from this
window you can see the broken down wagon which long ago he used to
haul ice from the river. he tells my wife and me that sometimes he feels
like his old wagon, missing wheels, boards missing, broken, or bowed
with time.

it is approaching 9 p.m. it is almost time to put my grandfather to bed.
he does not walk anymore. he has to be lifted from his wheelchair onto a
small hospital bed which barely seems present in a room that used to be
full of my abuelo and his history. when i was young he had a cabinet full
of rifles, pistols, and a sword from the spanish-american war. i admired
the 30.30, the magnums, the .32 beretta pistol, the massive sword which
seemed to weigh more than the entire room. his room seems smaller now.
the bed barely taking up space next to the north wall, the gun cabinet,
unlocked, empty except for the dust and various canes. it was not always
this way.

when i was young i would ride my bike the ¼ mile west to my
grandparents to chop wood for their wood stove. it was one of those
chores a kid does because he is a kid, not because he can chop wood
worth a darn. my abuelito could chop wood better than any man i have
ever seen. holding the wood block with his left hand, his right arm
ascending with a double adze blade, seven pounds, just above his head
and then dropping quickly like a blinking eye, inches away from the
fingers of his left hand, the log splitting perfectly, one blow. chopping
wood is one of those talents which is almost lost to the world, save for
memory.

he was rarely home, always driving his ford truck to some camp, some mountain. it is difficult to see him without motion. he is a nicer man now, but something in me longs for the meaner abuelito who struck fear in me as i admired him. i don't know, really, how to remember him, or if i should just know him as he is now. to remember or to know. perhaps both.

so here is how i will remember this place. just before dark with the sky blueing to black, my abuelito in a wheelchair, strong except for his legs. this kitchen with scuffed linoleum, my abuelito at his same spot, the head of the table, the empty chair to his left, my grandmother's place, empty for seven years now. the water from the well has always been cold and sweet. the window has always had a view of the vega, corral, the broken wagon at the bottom of the hill. there are only juice glasses in the cabinet; i leave the water running as i drink four glasses. my abuelito is behind me and to my left. he asks me if i remember this place, living here, my abuelita who always baked bread on friday. i finish my last glass of water, turn the faucet shut. i turn to my grandpa, knowing that i will always remember this place. "yes" i say, and for a while this is when the room becomes silent, the night finally wins and it is time for bed.

january with long shadows

we wait out
september rain
in a church with a tin roof
a thousand angels i say
running all at once

leaking roof
into old coffee can
at rear of the church
tin metronome
keeping beat
to a sermon on the devil
which is not
loud enough
to overcome the rain

january
Michele drives
sun in our eyes
hers focused
like purple fields

she turns north
onto old road to
ortiz cemetery

long shadows
a breeze we feel
but do not see
we visit her abuelita
new headstone
smiling picture at center
remember her
lessons on
family history
this one married that one
we are cousins to the first
they had three kids
second one died of a

burst appendix
the two girls
married brothers
from san miguel
they are related
to your mom
in the end
we are all cousins

my own abuelita
a shadow away
distant at winter sunset
a dormant grass
rust red
beside her settling grave
a sinking wound
after seventeen years
i barely remember
that far back
i pray
this red grass
was there then too

then my tio Willie
who drove a school bus
subtraction tells us
it has run without him
for nine years

every morning
a yellow bus
passes our house
i think of him
before the sun rises

my mother in law
remembers
my tio taking
the basketball team
to cotopaxi

his grandson Manuelito
did not have shoes
he loved that kid
drove that bus to cañon city
and bought him a pair

like rain
i do not know
what a september church
in a meadow
has to do with
january
is it about shadows
longer in winter
how i wait
for them
to form

the mortality of grass

the grass knows
    i
cannot   make the
       rain
warm
    or cultivate memories
like a
       spring plow
   heaven's
eternal   bruise
     is dark
   with anonymity
     turned and twisted
like Dali's clock
    where
     time
      is
    suspended
    in
    the brief
pitter splat
  of rain

oh
the grass knows
it
is versed
on
mortality
seeped
with
all
those
green
lessons
that cannot
escape dirt
i
feel
the
rain
now
i have
made the
rain
turn
warm
within
my
palm
and
tricked
death
to
let   me   stay

upon seeing the stars in a new way

he was tall and rocked back and forth when he drove. i know little of him, great grandfather, Juan Sanchez. i know he could irrigate and farm better than any man in mogote, perhaps better than any man in the valley. i know him because of the stories. he showed up one day at my parent's home; my mom and dad had just married. they had nothing, really, to show for their new marriage. this is the story i heard. my grandpa John shows up at the door one day. there is no mention of what he was driving or if he rocked back and forth the entire way to denver. he comes to the door with grandma Becky. they plan on staying. my parents have very little but they welcome them, the travelers from el valle de san luis who had come north. here is how my parents got their first t.v. Juan and Rebecca charged it to their wards card, and that is how it happened. this in itself is not such a great story; i know this. but the way Juan has come to me ever since is the way the story should work itself out.

they are always together my great grandpa John and grandma Becky. i never knew him, but my grandma i knew until i was in my teens. she slept most often, already old, tired, in the back room of her daughter's house, my abuelita's. but there were days, often when it was cold and nobody wished to be outside, when she would rise from her bed of springs and lumps with its many many blankets. she would rise and begin walking toward the front door. she would walk east, almost instinctively. sometimes she would make it quite far, other times we caught her on the dirt road just outside the house. we would ask her *"grandma where are you going?"* *"home"* she would reply *"pa mi casa."* what innate star directed her i will never know, what sense of judgment pointed her in the the right direction, toward a house twenty years abandoned. *"Juan me esta esperando,"* she would say. he had died in 1962 of a heart that no longer worked. we told her once that he had died *"many years ago"* we said. she did not know how to react, but could only remember him living, farming, strong. that was the last time we told her that he had died. we didn't want to see her scared in all her wrinkles, weak in her thin legs which moved in short steps. later we would tell her *"grandpa will be here soon."* she would wait with her memories and eventually fall asleep for days at a time.

so now i am twenty-eight, a writer now. Michele and i have moved back
to the valley from what seemed like a long way away. i thought of Juan
Sanchez while i was away, but he is stronger here, in the fields i cut for
my brother and father. he is strongest in the mornings on the empty
roads filled with pot-holes. it is here that i remember that he died in 1962.
can you miss a man you never knew? did i really ever leave this place? or,
did i wait patiently like my grandma Becky for the place to come to me.
my patience fulfilled in a way hers never quite was.

i thought of both of them my first night back. saw their skinny figures in
the stars, the grass that grew high this year. i had always wanted to return
to my home, like my grandma Becky on those winter mornings opening
the chain link gate, shuffling east in her bathrobe and thick slippers, her
white hair in a braid. moving in the direction the compass cannot define,
home.

i think of Juan and Rebecca showing up at a door one day, to stay. the t.v.
they charged was not important, but then again it was just that. "here's a
t.v." they must have said. here's a story you can tell your youngest, the one
who will never know me, but will remember my generosity. so it is, here
on this empty road lined by fields thick with hay.

a letter to guillermo, having missed his call

dear Guillermo
i have been waiting for just such an occasion to write you
a good snow
the flakes fat and wet
the earth silent
south and east of me
situate yourself
the sky to my left is the color of smoke from a house burning in autumn
if a person could get past the image of the man
in the gray jacket with his pants rolled above his work boots
past the image of the man shaking his head
it would be quite beautiful this sky and that burning house

i want you to know that i appreciated the call from you and Cynthia
i was sorry to have missed it
though i cannot say that i would have been one for talking
i feel better now
about all that has happened
at some point there was a part of me that took its final breath
at 1:35 p.m on february 15TH with my abuelito
a deep final breath
as though we were both intending to go under water
i miss my abuelito
and think of him as often as 100 students and four classes will allow
i suppose my fear came/comes from a place that is like inspiration
after it has walked into memory
but i read daily
and find great comfort in Walt Whitman
who believed that every soul was beautiful
that the soul was always beautiful
i can see now
why you would want him to lead you through Dante's inferno
though i do not wish fire for anyone
especially that man shaking his head at the beginning of this letter
what has fort collins and the months
since i saw you last offered in terms of life
my wish is that you are well and writing long poems with words like drums

Michele is improving daily from her long month
everyone has noticed a color in her skin that was not there before
the cyst they removed had been stealing from her body for some time
and we that love her and are around her every day
did not notice the paling of her skin
but now she is back with us
and we realize that we were not observant enough
i can only say that i
the poet who is supposed to notice things
did not see summer leave her face
nor did i notice the blank paleness that crept in
i have made a vow to be more observant and to remember better
people at their best
Michelle too was happy to hear from you and Cynthia and has relayed to me
the subtleties of both your voices and what they meant
she says her thanks through these words and i write them for her

i believe it is now sometime of 7:00 p.m.
the sky is entirely black
the moon and stars have no address in our southern sky
do you know if orion is still out there tilted in the west
hunting through the sky
or has he gone to his home in another hemisphere
i must be more observant
and take note of my friends more often
those real like yourself
and those cold and untouchable miles upon miles away in the sky
by now you have probably grown tired
of me mentioning venus to you and in relation to you
but you must know as i do
that she is blazing in the west early in the evenings
though tonight everyone is resting
while the snow returns like the march snows i used to pray for
the very same snow my brother and i would work in as we fed the sheep
my brother left-handed Andrew
is sad now without my abuelito
his cries of *my grandpa, my grandpa*
and his tears that betrayed him the fighter
are still haunting me
i always knew that my abuelito loved him best
that Andrew loved him best

but i cannot bring myself
to see my brother sad in the eyes
my abuelito's house empty
"tonight i can write the saddest lines"
somehow that line makes even more sense now
do i always write to you with sadness in my voice
that used to be Ramon Fernandez' job
my sounding board when i thought that words were becoming extinct
thank you for being that too

well Guillermo i will say goodbye for now
as the cd in the stereo plays its last song
something about pretty lies
the snow is good for me
i will watch it until sleep comes or until it turns itself to cloud
and moves like smoke over the sangre de cristos
do you think that the snow is always beautiful
that all snow is beautiful
that Whitman might think it to be like the souls in leaves of grass
goodnight amigo stay warm
adios,
a.

fences

like a frost
of stars
touchable and cold
on a winter night

the diamonds
of broken wine bottles
beneath limping
poles of cedar

the thwumm of its voice
the rider-less tractors
who wait like thursday
beyond rusted fingers

catorce canciones por seis cuerdas

I.
sometimes the earth burns
flames leap across rivers
both sides burn
but in the water
even the bear waits
patient   wet   alive

II.
having offended the gods so beautifully
a banished queen eternally upside down
rises near the moon watching
the dark earth turn and turn
her kingdom randomly lit
she must think the earth is made of mirrors

III.
on sunday we pray for rain
we pray and pray in the chords
of a guitar and a single shallow voice
carried in the stained glass
tonight if God is willing
i will dream of trees

IV.
this apple
i weighed in my palm
yellow and red freckled
with a blazing red swell
must have instinctively leaned its body
toward sweetness

V.
behind tumacacori mission
the infant Juanita Alegria is buried
behind tumacacori mission
with its falling walls and brackish water
Juanita Alegria has rested since 1916
who of her family still visits

VI.
on the last day of may
Mary visits Elizabeth and John leaps
within her belly at the sound of Mary's voice
and the coming of his cousin
so too perhaps   did the round eyed boy
Andres

VII.
sometimes the song of our life
is as permanent
as the passing of wet feet
on hot cement
are we moving
or disappearing

VIII.
when there is still a small chance
the referees will always start the clock early
but Tony Quintana runs down the sideline
clock evaporating like the final syllables
of a rosary   hail Mary full of   he gets a step
grace

IX.
jupiter and io are the first visible dancers
in the june dusk
tomorrow it will rain for Michele's birthday
many thanks that God and the earth
have made their peace
a wednesday

X.
there is birdsong in the still moist air
the sweet june scent of
our collective memory
last night   nine puppies were
born in a dark culvert
'para sanar los corazones heridos'

XI.
another wednesday
Juan Diego is canonized
there are conch horns in the cathedral
quetzal feathers in the cathedral
all of tepeyac is red
with roses

XII.
sometime later this year
our children will not live to be born
their ascension will be called
a baptism of desire
we will bury them
beneath a cedar tree

XIII.
there is a rock wall
a small tree grows from the rock
could it be   yes let's let
that tree growing from this
loom made of rock
may that tree stand for love

XIV.
God maker of the sky that does not rain
God of judgments please be kind
to this one and also that one
show mercy for fourteen and all those other angels
we send we send we send and send
show mercy for the song that plays

elegy on spring and other losses

this place is where
the bible used to come true
pero esta primavera
we live only with the flames
of fields burning
and grass that does not return
in a spring that will not forgive us

we do not love
the blank blue eye of sky
we pray daily
for rains that do not come
we pray for our lambs
to make it through their
malnourished and bloated spring

so when the word comes
that Brenda died in seasons
her kidneys finally failing
three days after
drinking prestone and tylenol
we barely question her methods
her poorest of suicides
the knowledge it brought
as her body began to quit
one organ after the next
Brenda conscious
of the spring
dying within us all

i picture her in the only
image i have of her
pregnant in my parents' living room
standing next to Kiko
asking for Kiko's pay a week early

Brenda slightly smiling
they leave happy
and this is the way
i'll remember her
until i see her son
fourteen years later
in an april morning silently driving sheep
from our haystack
as his father drives
the truck into the bosque to feed
i ask myself why he is not in school
i don't see his pregnant mother
i don't see his unborn body
leaning against our table
he walks too slow
and the sheep leave the pila
more out of habit than his urging

may 21st
i hear about his sister
who can't stop crying
his mother
who died on a previous thursday
and the body that will not
arrive from albuquerque
she will be cremated
and we understand that is how
everything must work this year
when the ditches did not rise above 17
and the meadows
dead cannot will themselves green
we are so used to fire forgiving the earth
burning the sin from our memory
but we cannot find
the part of the song
that plays even in silence
the dry well of the human heart
the dropped stone we understand too well

the quiet baby that exits
while the crying
so very alive baby remains
not even the mountains can save us
from a sky that seems dead
from the flames of a burning meadow
from green that will not come
from a quiet boy
on an april morning
silenty driving sheep from a haystack
whose green
is the last remnant
of what might be possible

love poem after a passing antelope

i have come
to one of the old campaderos
there is this voice
that sounds like a breeze
and a red earth
impossibly clinging
to the last hours before dusk

from where i stand
in the dark circle
of a long ago removed corral
there is nothing but east ahead of me
and some faint image
a mirage of five antelope
not really running
but gliding windlike
over the sage and volcanic rock

there is something blind inside of me
like a love poem
some pit of the stomach uneasiness
that is almost beautiful
i cannot imagine
this place more clearly
than it is painted here today
clouds their bodies full of rain
resting their tiredness
on the sangre de cristos

something out here
on this loma
is trying to remember me
my scent downwind
in some cautious place
that only moves a few steps at a time
then grazes grazes
looks up and cannot remember

today out in the hills
that beg for rain
beneath the passing river noise
of a jet unzipping
the blue and gray sky
i am almost
face to face with you now
this singing wind
a Whitman soul that sends out
"filament filament filament"

you are thin legged cautious
winter has treated you well
can i call you love
like a memory of grazing sheep
or are you something else
beautiful and singular
like a smile

i love you silent saturday
and something yes something
very old and repetitive loves me too
more gently than the earth
loves rain
more spiritually than a solitary tree
loves wind
more slowly than the moon
loves clouds
you passing thing
like 8 a.m. on a wednesday
the last of your voice
i love you
like something green and windy
in the first days of spring

horse poetry

hooves
pounding
the igneous ribs of my rock

waiting
for the first lunge
the earth coming up

gathering sweat
in its own momentum
white like sun

frothy at the neck
nostrils flare
hot and dry

the earth recoils and spins dancing to the rhythm

of the horse heart

chinelas

sawmill whistle
far off blowing
like the sadness
of a single church bell
while transplanted
sawmill workers
from north carolina
sit in the only bar
that will take them

the man
in gold buckled dress shoes
a giant with
sockless feet callused at the ankles
his shift over
with the sad bell
from eight hours before
has made the bar in the hum of
the neon beer lights his
and he will not leave

the bosses
½ block down
in their own bar
cannot hear him
the voice which
hates the homes of scrap lumber
the railroad tracks outside
his splintered door
loose hanging there
like the teeth
of the town marshall
out on the floor
the chinela man fists still balled
stands over him
the sun barely in the sky
burning

a call over the new
short wave radio
'sheriff there is a man
who has gone crazy
at the chirinola bar'

my gunless abuelito
walks through the open summer door
confronts the man
who says he will not move

abuelito walks into the bar
twenty years removed from texas
he remembers the signs
no mexicans or dogs allowed
the similar sun its balled fist
that takes him from
railway to railway
cleaning chicken coops
for a hot meal
and the cc bosses
in the shade of their straw hats
the twenty-five cents per day wages
jobs reserved for mexicans
streets, bars, theatres
not for them
the leftover grief
of not belonging

they stand there
one man in boots
his shoulders thick
from the potato fields
the other feet bare
in his black chinelas
he is too much with this place
his falling home of wood scrap
his splintered door
the sawdust between his toes
the town that will not have him
the cold at this altitude
his sockless feet
his turned up chinelas

they have passed that place
where talking can work
abuelito knows why
a man in a segregated bar
must swing first
he is that same man in a place
where time does not exist
the anger it holds
thick hands of his memory
what the sun can do to a man
when he holds it in his fist

one man falls
the men lining the bar
return to their drinks
ignoring the far off whistle
the town barely noticing
the man with the gold buckled shoes
being put in the back of the plymouth squad car
the last of the sun
tolling like a bell

into the leftward way home

there is a sense
to turning left
on the old roads that run
into the ancestry of horse chasers and vaqueros

raised
from this land
of piñon trees
and clay bordered sage
grows the womb
of spanish rivers
and the sustenance of maize

we are baptized
to the secrets
of God's symmetrical mesas
which are passed down
as ceremoniously as rain
by sun baked tradition

there is a sense
to turning left

it is written in these shadowed cliffs
which surround
this leftward llano

where shielded time
and ancient roads
send me quickly
toward my home

hometown

southbound
where clouds gather in reunion
the thunderheads
shaped like horses
their necks - bruised and fat with rain

a visual circe
that sucks me in
past the peaks that stand at attention
way deep
into the murky run-off
which gurgles promises
of people waiting

like Jose Maria
the diplomat
who agrees with everyone
because his brain is pickled
and his bloated skin
is the pungent pink of tokay wine

like Tony Loco
who traded his easel
for a bag of dope
and a job painting fences

old men who chase echoes
young women
who dream of becoming hairdressers

dinner will be waiting
my arrival has been rumored
ever since my departure

"he won't last" they said
as i fled in defiance
and now
as my radio whispers defeat
i roll on

serenade for life at dusk

wooden flute sings
sings
i
say

like a mystery
unfolding
in
the
grass

sings

sings to the owl
perched
on the
barren
finger
of a cottonwood

sings

sings
to the thin dusk
collecting
in the
red
walled
canyon

asking the owl
to return
a resurrection with the sky
and the day moon
of the east
as witness

the song
the oncoming darkness
the earth

sings

dancing quietly
beneath
the wings
of the
owl

as orion falls

i will begin with our unborn children
the ones i tell Michele will look
to us like the season's first snow
resting beneath the burned trees
of last season's fires

later i tell her that our children
will be like the first time we saw the pacific
i only see them in symbol
each time they are something wet
after too much dryness
i love them already
so we name them
Amalia and Andronico
and i finally dream Amalia into existence
she has enormous brown cheeks
her hair is soft as
the underside of a bird's wing
and her smile is like the train
coming into town
after Sam Duran tucked the ball under his arm
one second on the clock
forty yards out and he begins to run
one tackle two   three broken
he scores and everyone for miles
is honking their horn
we are waving to one another   the whole town
smiling as if it were 1977
everything is   i feel young again
and then the train begins to whistle
her heart boiling with the fire of
soft black coal   legs uncoiling coiling recoiling
as she eases into the depot
her whistle loud and unexpected
is what we are all feeling
and this is the way my daughter
our daughter will smile at us
when everything is   young
again

even train whistles are short lived
save them in memory
but their reality
the loud part of the metaphor
the consolation for the sad part of us
cannot last

i am writing about the possibility
of a daughter whose smile i've only dreamt once
and less than twelve hours
after Sam began running we are sad again

he was 17
i didn't know him
his mother is a good person
i didn't know him
the last time i saw him
he was smiling
he had red hair
write it down
he drove a tan escort
he was smiling
his hair was red in all the hours of light
write it down
Chris Ruybal   his name
no one knows why he did it
there are others

Laverne's liver fails blood flows from her ears

Brenda drinks prestone

Bino's mother asks three times
for a poem about her son
tell everyone how he was a good guy
rescued Ana from the swing
where her hand was caught
picked up my hat after that sixth grade fight

write it down

how Eddie made you laugh kool-aid all over his family
and how you saw him twenty years later
cutting through the alley
on his way to the liquor store
write it down
how he died and you didn't even know he was sick

there is a list of reasons why
i shouldn't dream my daughter
but she is my snow in the burned trees
the pacific after the desert
i haven't told you yet
she is orion at 1:54 a.m.
a sunday in september
on the dark road home from albuquerque
she is reason to breathe
to whistle unexpectedly

lists i say
Ronnie always smiling
and the wednesday before thanksgiving
we are all sad again
no one knows

Vanessa
who went for a drive before she was 16
the roadside burned
a cottonwood caught fire
her locker had apologies taped to it
lists of names
and my aunt wants
me to write about people who are alive
another woman asks me
why i am always writing
about someone that
no one gives a shit about

i can only tell her that
it is my job
to write about the someones

this poem will be long
the names real
the list partial

i want for this to be a love poem
i don't want the young white woman
to smile an i'm sorry smile
in my direction when
i tell her i'm from antonito

here is a story i remember
it is about love
sometimes it becomes a metaphor
for what love really is
i am six years old
my abuelito driving us toward the cow camp
we drop down into ortiz
her old houses silent in the orange part of the day
the first house on our left
becomes my abuelito's story
the mesa 300 yards east of the house
becomes its conclusion
"there" he says
it is a chimney missing bricks at the top

i think the Durans have always lived there
one in particular must have been beautiful
surrounded by flowers
one tree in the yard
dress of well pressed flour sacks
her hand raised waving
to the man who loved her
who daily would drop from the sky
his plane like a bird wrapped in thunder
his engine growling out
what the silent wings could not say

there in the thick part of the summer
in the red part of the day
the two of them must have been
a wonderful metaphor
for what i am trying to say

Ortiz would profess his love
his plane buzzing her house
shaking los santos en las ventanas
until they became tired of his love

maybe it was their jealousy
something about the sky
that their ceramic smiles were hiding

most people say it was a gust of wind
i think it was too much weight
the plane dipping farther toward the ground
was not an act of nature
it was the weight of what would have to carry us
something like the persistence of the santos
waiting for heaven in a north facing window
brought the plane down
the landing gear knocking the brick teeth
from the root of the house
Ortiz losing control
the woman with the flour sack dress
dropping her hand slowly with the red plane
until both were finally resting
one shaking   the other burning
in the black rocks of the mesa

now we must find other examples of our love
something that will not burn itself away

Alberto died of parkinsons
he taught me how to irrigate
every time i see a shovel worn smooth with use
or smell a flooded alfalfa field's sweet scent
recuerdo
acequias of cold water
a field and an old man
Alberto
steady with his shovel
who saved me from the wet rattlesnake
under the tarpolio
the snake striking once
at the air above my right foot
the shovel coming down on its neck
Alberto Gallegos saved my life
taught me to irrigate
these are the same things
write about
the worn shovel
the scent of an alfalfa field
return the favor

Manuel Ortiz

did the impossible
found water by using a bent willow

i remember the well diggers
a man in a white shirt
with a machine that sent sound into the earth
telling everyone to dig and so we did
120 feet down there was water
we tapped it   pumped it for about a month
and then it went dry
the man in the white shirt
with his poetry machine
had only been partially right
so we called Manuel
my abuelito's good friend
who arrived in his white ford
his black dog sitting in the passenger seat
he never went anywhere without that dog
they only had each other

Manuel Ortiz
his body bent by the immeasurable weight
of the willow in his hands
walked around as though he had lost something
a small knife in the dust
a wedding ring in the cut weeds
a small voice in the earth
until finally he stopped
the willow quivering and bending
innately toward the water it believed
could save it and us
and then we began to dig again

40 feet down
water flowing over rocks made of candy and ice
never going dry
though it sputtered this summer
barely enough to cook with and drink from
Manuel Ortiz   water witch
dying in the driest month
finally answering the voice
deep in the sweet cold part of the well

i want for this poem to be about living too
there are 112 lambs in the bosque
they run through the march morning
moving like water
running in a bosque
alive and together
tails wagging in the cold air
before the sun rises

i want you to see my gente
they are cottonwoods
wild and bent
at beautiful and dangerous angles
we are not straight stands
of thin skinned aspen
or broad pine and spruce

we live near rivers
our scars evident
we have branches that turn on themselves
we are impossible to imagine
but our sombra is ancient

the bark of our bodies thicker than wind
our bent arms swaying
in the windy spring
the force of that wind
multiplied by our persistence
should equal something
like our death
something like a constant falling

yet here on the bosque floor
in the thickest parts of the shadows
there are cottonwood blossoms forming
waiting to drift
people soft as snow
speaking quietly about
all there is to live for

i want this poem to be about seeing
about the alamo that does fall in the wind
and how the others protect it
in their gnarled way
and pray for it
with their soft spring blossoms
which fall into the
exposed heart of the broken tree

el pescador

i see the red willow
bent over the river
and it reminds me of you
the fisherman Cristobal

i still fish these waters
long after you tore away
from all those river dreams
like the sun tears away from the dew
too soon gone
and a dry wind hums through the trees

i always knew
that nothing scared you
the only thing that could touch you
was yourself

i saw your little brother
and wondered why he didn't fish
wondered why i called him by your name
why the willows sagged like memory
asking questions

i cast into the smooth green water
letting the hook sink deep
as it scrapes over the rocky bed

nothing to be caught
everything finally done

coyote

is was easy to blame coyote
because coyote drinks whiskey
it makes for poor memory
and that's what coyote likes best

so when they asked him
about all the nice homemade girls
some real guitar pickers among them

he said

i only buy them drinks
for the pleasure of their leather tongued company
hell
i'd buy the whole joint a round
if only they would talk

so coyote
sticks mostly to himself
so as not to offend the wolves or prairie chickens
and that is why
they convicted coyote of stealing
the curvy hitcher
that had the elk hopping fences

they mailed him
to a ZIP somewhere
outside of the northern lights
sentenced for two to six
to howl at the moon
and never again
take his whiskey sips

a letter to Sibley from this place

dear George,

here is this struggle, my struggle to write about a place when all i do is write about this place. Some part of me feels like all you have to do is press play and i will begin again in some innate migration to the llanos, mountains, churches and rivers that form my home. i suppose it is no accident that i chose the word migration. my people came to my valley home and lands of new mexico over 400 years ago and have been stealing or stolen from ever since.

i tell my students that we are by nature a migratory people. our own migration is like orion's, the constellation just now back in our night, and his winter journey through the sky. he begins himself, tilted in the east, lying on his side and moves slowly upright in the southern sky before falling again on his side in the west. and then there is my own abuelito who personified this for me, who fell into his western sky on february 15th at 1:35 p.m. by now you must be wondering what my many loose connections, stars, migration, religion, family are trying to do here. ultimately, they must be together and will be my place.

George, here is how the connections come to me. i am six years old and my parents have moved us to pueblo, where my dad has found work. every weekend, and i mean every weekend, we load our caprice classic and we drive south to this place that is ours. sometimes my older brothers have football games and we leave after, our headlights cutting through the early morning of a road filled with pot-holes, so that we can pull into the driveway of my boyhood home at three in the morning. later, at six a.m., my father wakes us so that we can begin the ranch work which has been neglected during the week. the story unfolds from there, packing up sunday evening and returning to pueblo and a house where we all do not fit, my brothers sleeping in the family room.

to me the idea of a place, a sense of place is somewhere we come back to at all costs and at all hours of the day or night. i think often of the monarch butterflies and their yearly migration to the south where they will finally rest in the mexican pines. i have heard that there are so many of them that the trees groan from the weight of so many butterflies, the thick branches bent toward the earth in supplication. here is the tragic part. every year fewer and fewer butterflies return to mexico. they are victims of pesticides, growth and too many cars, much like us.

i mention the butterflies because they remind me of my town and how many of us return despite the poverty, and like the monarchs fewer and fewer make the journey with each passing generation. my town is still poor, though every year the river canyon west of my home is gobbled up by homes made of beautiful scraps. the lumber which goes into the homes is standard grade, the same stuff that clogs canyons and shorelines everywhere so that someone can have a view. the scraps, those are measured in human terms. for the most part these transplants buy only the necessities from my town, gas and fishing licenses. we see very little of the wealth that grows three stories high on a ridge where pine and aspen used to mingle. we are a beautiful people that too many think of as scrap.

so back to the butterflies, may my God bless them and their journey. may this same God bless orion and all the rest of us who travel so that we may return and rest in the warm trees that are innately part of us. all this rambling George, and essentially what i'm saying is that a place defines us because the soul and the home are synonymous.

one last thing amigo, earlier i mentioned my abuelito and his passing. his star is somewhere beyond the san juans' grasp, fading slowly from this hemisphere and brilliantly into another. i mention him because i miss him and because i believed, and to a certain extent still do, that he is permanently a part of this place, my home, a mountain range away from yours. i never got to say goodbye to him, though i was at his bedside on that february afternoon when it seemed even the sheep in the field below his home stopped moving. the only thing in the air was his last breath and the mumbled prayers of someone speaking too fast in spanish.

so you see George, there is no sense to goodbyes because our human mind will not let go what it knows will return. i see my abuelito at the table playing solitaire, chopping wood, driving off to the sheep camp or simply standing there broad shouldered. this too, memory, is our place, and this round home we call earth, she disappears from herself and from us at times but returns in whatever positions are native to her and our memory. these canyons that wrinkle her and the butterflies that fan her and rest in her hair keep coming, migrating toward us and through us or perhaps it is the other way around. we cannot say goodbye to our places, no matter how they change, we must always return to them. George we make each place our own by the things we return to it, living or remembered.

much peace to you and your own place with its migrations uniquely yours. please do share.

be well

your friend
a.

clouds like horses

i am three generations
of clouds like horses
arching muscles
tattooed to the sky
by the brown bicepped machismo
of the man
i call abuelito
who wears a callus of sun
thick on his hands

the story of every scar
written in the jagged lines of his knuckles
that worked the potato farms
for twenty-five cents a day

a bruise left on his memory
from swinging a twelve pound sledge
for a man who called him a dirty mexican

i am a man like my father
strong as clouds
thunder built up
black in their bellies
the bulging veins
tell the cuento
about the big mormon
who beat him when he was sixteen
for daring to date the wrong girl
breaking his skin
until the bitterness lingered in his blood

i am three generations
of clouds like horses
unharnessed
rolling over the llano
a promise rumbling
that they will live on

adios prayer for goodbyes

dios por vida
why does the sign of the cross
always feel like goodbye
some chain link gate half open
where the cows can get in
and eat my abuelita's flowers

por vida
i hate that joke
that feels like goodbye
where the pope tells me Pancho Villa
and that other mexican
to get the fuck out of here

when that man
told me i should teach spanish
not english
because i was fluent in spanish
that was like a goodbye
until a fourth of july horserace
when la palomina outran
his thoroughbred
adios cabron
i'm fluent in english too

in the name of the father the son and
pray for us sinners now and at the hour
when he ascended into heaven
and is seated at the right hand
no i don't like that joke
where Jesus is mexican
because he is thirty-three
still lives with his parents
and believes his mother
is a virgin

holy water
this hurts
like a death the day
after valentines day
dear lord pray
that no one i love
dies in winter
dear lord pray for everything
and save someone today
maybe someone who feels
that prayers are farewells

song that Julia asks for

in truth   Bino
the poem began
before your mother asking
for these words
not a repetition of your failings
her eyes tell me
no one has forgotten them

you come to me in california
in the pacific which Pablo loved
in new york
outside a building whose bricks
always look wet
in a poem about Billie Holiday
where everyone stops breathing
in a crowd that wanders
blankly when the lights allow

here is that truth again
after weeks away
from july's daily rains
i miss the clouds
their heavy bruises
bleeding across the mojave
receding into the wave formed rocks
of the Navajo nation
breaking   finally on the san juans
and now i'm listening
again to the poets
talking about the danger
of using the word beautiful
truth   there is very little beauty
in a liver that no longer works
yet   Bino
thank you for picking up my hat
after that sixth grade fight

california new york and colorado
repeat themselves
when the pacific's
watery horses come ashore
when pairs of yellow butterflies
hover flutter dance
over a puddle of water
when there is a
possibility of rain

i cannot shake you
you haunt me
like a horse in a winter field
like a mother
who outlives her son
like a sky that is not
the sun's work
like purple things that bloom
outside an empty house

a letter to K. translating spanish

i think it is interesting that you would mention the valley sky, breath and cold now that orion is wildly tilted in our eastern winter sky. he is my favorite constellation though i do not know what he could be hunting in a sky so welcoming.

recently i looked over some of my very old and not so good poems and noticed that i mentioned sky almost instinctively. i was fascinated with clouds, rain, snow and other things aviary like our owl. later, i looked at the new stuff and noticed that the sky had left the poems. there was no mention of the fingernail moon, the clouds that arrive already bruised in late summer. orion, every night, reminds me that the sky is what makes the valley. at first i thought it was the mountains, the winter blanca, crestone and the san juans. at one point i thought it was religion that defined the valley. these things are still very much a part of me and this place Michele and i again call home.

the sky though. the mornings are my favorite. sunrise and all its shades of blues, blacks and reds. i said once that the sky in the mornings is a malignant blue. i don't think people understood what i meant by that   malignant is such a negative word even for a sky that is immune to negativity. i did not mean that the sky would die of some disease, though some think it might, but rather that it grows from itself, multiplies in ways a pen, brush or imagination cannot fathom. often we do not know why things grow inside us. the sky knows itself very well i think. it grows with purpose.

so every night as orion lies there in the winter east, i breathe a few visible breaths in his direction. i watch as the vapor ascends without the reservations of gravity. i can see the silhouetted hills and mountains against the light of the stars, millions of them. without the sky there would be no mountains. i think maybe your student might have meant *poner*. as in to put light into a person's shoes. perhaps he meant for someone to walk like the stars, across the dark sky with all their lit shoes and bright eyes. *para poner la luz en tu zapatos*. that is quite nice.

i will tell our owl, Michele's good friend with the very white wings that stretch into the abovementioned sky, to look out for you and your good husband. so that you will know, she flies over an earth which is mostly brown, though it looks gold when the light is right.   just the other day the owl flew over a white earth, and that night as the frost formed on the wire fences around our home, in the headlights of our vehicle, the crystals of ice looked like stars, touchable and cold. the sky caught my breath that night, and orion did not hunt.

adios
your friend
a.

the absent heart
for Amalia or Andronico

a small piece of paper
something the size of an ant's heart
falls from the book
onto my bare chest streaked in rays
of december sun
reflecting through a southern window
it falls on my heart
both fall and continue
on my heart

i give you back small heart
to the book
to your mother's wish
to your father's silence
i give you back smaller heart
to your still shadow in the center
to your warm and resting body
the absent heart
the song Michele fills in
on a day for miracles
of sight and healing
look
someone is building a house
in the winter

heard poem

autumn will cure me
if it does not
i will die when everything
is cool and gold

the body is fourteen stars

i tell Michele i want a space pen for my birthday
so i can then write   upside down
but really i want for her to find her grief in the piano keys
and lightly touch it   note by note
a mother's soft hands
tracing her child's face

but after that
when grief is as real as
fire three feet from your window
i want her to burn everything into melted glass
something liquid   painful and beautiful
something like a christmas light
that begs you to grab it even as it burns you

the body's grief
is the fourteen stars of orion's body
there are more than that
yet i always manage   because i'm grieving too
to only count 14 stars
his red shoulder   blue foot
the three bright angels at his belt
perfect cells their bubble form in a mother's womb
and then i count the faint heart
the dimmest star
the heart is the faintest star
the one that keeps betraying us
re-dieing every time someone
says pregnant or ultrasound

now that i've counted six of the fourteen angels
i want the other eight
Meissa the hunter's head
Bellatrix his shoulder and Saiph his other foot
horsehead nebula of sword where three give birth to millions
and two unfertilized stars one above his blue foot
the other below and right of his belt
i'd like for those eight to quit their counting
had they been born
i would have clipped their nails
into perfect slivers of moon

and they must know we love them same as the six
a small comfort in a fire
the family photo saved
while the home returns to ashes
this love
this baptism of desire
is where i begin
to equate stars with eternity

therefore in this equation
eight plus six equals fourteen
and fourteen crosses of oil on the breasts of fourteen babies
and fourteen handfuls holy water on fourteen heads
equals seventy multiplied by two parents praying
is 140 multiplied by the variable x where x=days since all were lost
and x = 180 but grows daily and in today's tally is 25,200
multiplied by the two that lived longest
is 50,400 added to the one
day in january where i dug one frozen grave
beneath one solitary cedar tree   all counted here
comes to 50,403 multiplied by beads on a rosary
not counting the glory be and the apostle's creed
equals 2,973,777 then again multiplied
by the number of rosaries prayed which also changes daily
bringing today's number of stars to 157,610,181
which is the hard number i believe many are looking for
to prove that pain is real
and that one does not visibly need to lose something
to begin counting and thus smooth rosary beads
with a mother's touch and therefore make
a body of fourteen stars eternal
therefore proving something   i.e. love like pain
is also eternal

now is when i realize
that we saved no photo from the burning
save for each other   two
my beautiful wife and i
where the i cannot ease the one remaining
so in the next room she is making the sounds
of fingers searching through sheet music in a wooden piano bench
and this is what i must take from this june night

where the moon is full
its blue hue fading through a southern window
onto this poem and that december

she's playing the piano again
something slow and cautious
i can tell she doesn't know her way
she is feeling the keys and not yet the song

the piano is part of it
this cautious hammering of notes
but you must understand
that orion was born to a family that could not have children
he was born from his father's wish
who on his birthday in june
wishes orion back from the 22nd of may
when he fell into another hemisphere
fell head first into another father's world
fell toward another father who despite december
loves winter more than summer because
the stars seem brighter
his unborn children more real

so on my birthday
i do want to be able to write upside down
and yes   this moon does keep marking
but what i really want
is for that dim heart
the faintest star to keep true in its flame
its baptism of desire
to burn and keep burning
to burn and
keep burning
thus continuing to burn
and burn and keep burning
so small loves
can be pulled from its flame
making ashes bearable

san acacio garage

metaphor of dirt   straw   water
human work
set solid
at llano's edge

a poet
someone with patience
for almost straight lines
must have made this their
three word poem
red lettering on plywood
a shouting sign
to no one passing through
SAN ACACIO GARAGE

the brown adobe garage
must handle the teacher
who says her language
is not diligent enough
forced into a lie
that thousands of adobes
handmade   human placed   mud mortared
are not diligent enough when compared
to new steel
and windows larger than
the moon fading through them

can this be reason enough to write
those three red words
which remind us
even empty garajes with
slanted light razoring
through cob-webbed windows are
human adobes

adobes   with missing teeth
adobes   that are lonely
adobes   that lose children before and after christmas
adobes   that had their rights purchased before they knew their rights

adobes   with water that doesn't flow
adobes   that get no mention
adobes   that don't read good books
adobes   that should learn english
adobes   that don't dare call themselves mexican
adobes   whose bodies are shaped by wine
adobes   with bells that don't ring
adobes   made new with paint and then condemned
adobes   made mostly of earth
adobes   whose sermons are on sin
adobes   whose savior fell three times before rising
adobes   who are mothers
adobes   who are fathers
adobes   of thinking stone
adobes   of forgetful wood
adobes   made of three red worded poems
adobes   that should be noticed
adobes   that do not fall when they are not
adobes   that do not wish their walls to glass
adobes   that do not wish themselves to steel because it is new
adobes   that are like a huge garaje in the tiniest town
adobes   that speak after their patria quits listening
adobes   that are heard even after the paper has sent letters of denial
adobes   that last forever
adobes   that sing old songs
adobes   that last because woman and man saw them from the earth
adobes   that last because someone saw fit to give them names

a letter to Sibley from the sovereign banks of the conejos

it is good to be writing again. the mountains have snow, the air is cold, the sun is shining. it is a good november day and i have been thinking of you and this idea of sovereignty, an almost foreign word here where there is so much poverty and most of us, to some degree, rely on a government, that mostly ignores us, to survive. i suppose the skeptic in me believes that the government wants its minorities that way, dependent, but i don't want this letter to be about bitterness. instead i want you to come to the river with me where we can talk about this beautiful wish, sovereignty. both words, river and sovereignty lead me to Gerald Arellano.

i looked up sovereignty in the dictionary. i was hoping for something that didn't mention autonomy, politics or governance. i was hoping because in terms of those words, antonito does not necessarily fit. in any of those arenas we are not heavy hitters. however, as of late, i've found that the dictionary is a place for discovery. i held out hope and there it was. the first definition. before autonomy, before body politic. there waiting for us on page 836 of my webster's seventh new collegiate was this definition. "supreme excellence or an example of it." it made reference to Shakespeare's *love's labor's lost* "*of all the complexions the cull'd sovereignty do meet in her fair cheek.*"

so with this i come to Gerald Arellano who has been haunting my poetry for years now. growing up in cañon, he was our nearest neighbor, about ¼ mile away to the east. for most people, Gerald would not come to mind as an example of supreme excellence. as men go, he had the basic features of a man but did not exude any other characteristics we think of when we say the word 'man.' he was a thin man, almost non-existent, his tall brown body racked with diabetes, alcoholism, drug abuse. he lived in an uninsulated trailer with his wife and daughter. later these two would die in the most horrible traffic accident i have ever seen. Gerald asked that i be one of the six that carried his daughter to her grave, but the tragedy of Gerald Arellano existed long before his family was taken from him. he did not work. their home had no running water, and to survive he waited for his welfare check. in his daily life he was not an example of supreme excellence.

usually around christmas, my abuelito would hire Gerald to do some work around the ranch. just some under the radar stuff paid in cash every weekend. we knew he wouldn't return after the first payday. we hired him anyway because my abuelito liked Gerald's father. i tell you all this because in the eyes of this nation and our community Gerald Arellano was close to worthless. Yet, as a boy i admired him more than any other man i knew. i believe in my God; i see him as loving, a presence, who despite the traumas of our lives, gives each of us a gift. a gift of supreme excellence.

one river, the conejos, which drops toward the rio grande, has a special place in my heart. it was on this river that i learned about supreme excellence. his name was Gerald Arellano. he died of his failings a few years back. he probably wasn't over forty years old. i failed to record the day, month and year of his passing, but this letter will serve as record that he was the greatest fisherman i have ever known.

as a young boy i would look east out of our living room window and wait for his thin ghostlike figure to emerge from his, weathered, white, trailer, rod in hand and move slowly north toward the river.

i had a dream about Gerald the other day. i had walked into a room where sadness was tangible, a thick humidity of despair. my dream saw Gerald and many others like him, and my dream told me to seek out their beauty. the dream asked me to save them with their own gift by using mine, these words.

and so i would wait for him to move north toward the river and i would run to stand by his side, my own fishing pole ready to mimic his cast, the holes, the retrieval of the lure. i was his mirror. everyone thought he was a bum, but he would catch 20, 30 fish. i would beg some from him to make four, enough for my mother, father, brother and myself. he always shared.

so what does any of this have to do with sovereignty? as a writer i must have faith that one human can represent all of us. Gerald Arellano is that for me. by all accounts he had nothing, and what little he had was taken from him at an intersection two miles up the road from his trailer. antonito, while she still has more than Gerald, has had many things taken from her. some are measurable as in acres and cubic feet of water. other losses are more discreet but just as devastating. to be sovereign, autonomous, self-governing, economically viable, free, each of us must realize our one gift. sometimes, if God and genetics are good there are many to choose from, but often there is just that one, the one that cannot be stolen because people don't look into the well past the water they have come to drink. each of us, each community despite circumstance or poverty must foster the one gift, the one resource, our one example of supreme excellence. if we do this sovereignty becomes easier. some may argue that setting the gift free opens it up to be stolen. i stood by Gerald's side, mimicked him to the smallest detail, used the same lures and equipment and still, twenty years later, i cannot match him.

many have suggested that gambling will save antonito. we have had enough of the odds. other communities are also expected to benefit from outside enterprise, whether it be ski slopes or cabins in a formerly pristine canyon. only your gift can save you, not what someone else says is the cure. to be sovereign we must realize our natural gifts and harvest them. we cannot be complacent or happy with the scraps of the american dream. we must let our excellence be our mark.

perhaps Gerald Arellano was a bum. he was beautiful too, excellent, supremely so, there on the conejos where this boy and maybe even the fish miss him. on the conejos he was free, autonomous, memorable, totally aware that some gifts cannot be purchased, stolen, neglected or lost. years later, i too realize something, only the beautiful parts of our existence can save us.

George, here's hoping that salvation of this sort finds each of us.

your friend,
a.

Satchel Paige: a postcard from coors field

the cut grass   hot dogs   and warm peanuts
have   by now   become cliché
if only this note could convey them
then perhaps you too would be here

i never played well or with much style
though there was a time
when i thought i was Satchel Paige
big chalk square on the side of our brown house
i tried to be Satchel
high kick   motion of a taut spring uncoiling

my father knows the game
quite a bat in his day
he tells me how the young Satchel was unhittable
how in his prime he had too much show for the show

how beautiful he must've been

these fellows who took the hill today
have neither the arm nor the style
at 42 he broke into the bigs after Robinson
pitched 'til he was 59
a young Satchel would have been a sight
to have seen those lily white jim crows
swing at the third and shake their heads

here's wishing you a day
filled with all the style of an old man
with a young arm
tomorrow there will be another game
and again i will think of you and Satchel Paige
his high leg kick and the angry noise his fastball must have made

adios, be well
your friend
a.

p.s.
ever noticed how baseball is a metaphor for everything, even history we
wished we could forget rather than regret?

a question of returning

is this possible
are migratory monarch butterflies
and a woman humming
only slightly out of tune
in the next room over
metaphors for the same thing
can there be too many words
in the trees
too many butterflies
in the mexican pines
resting with the sum
of north american summers
under their wings

is that really the tree groaning
the weight of all that airiness
creaking in a soft breeze
her limbs praying
head down in a mexican summer
God bless those butterflies
and what is left of memory
that vague unpunctuated question
the bulk of it saying
i miss you
come back soon

and here too is a question
can purple survive in january
with her broken summer
because this is something
of an attempt
to absolve myself
an apology to the woman
i spoke of harshly
for not returning calls
her silence
later i find is for the child
the one she waited for
never born

must i apologize
this too is a question
must i
for all the things
i said to myself

and and yes and
why does this man
keep coming to me
this boxer i never knew
the local men said he was mean
this was his compliment
and his curse
he took his he
took this question of his
to his wife's face
her bruises
a love divisible by zero
and and yes and one
day she killed him

so you see the question
is this
at what point
after our gift kills
or begins to kill us
is it something else
ceasing like spring
to be a compliment

and no one
not even the wife
who is killing you
not even the gray days
that own what is left of you
yes no one
not even
the silence left of zero

or the heavy butterflies
in the mexican pine trees
can answer this
the eternal part of the question
which ceases so that
it can return
a child to the womb

if you must

sell self selfishly
to pursue another lover
rapacious salacious geishas   lost agnostic
methedrine magazine children praying

amen again
because muse must disgusted
fall all away into sinewy torment rent
of love where therein form transformed

into oozy nothingness
regresses slack-jawed jig-sawed hallmark
Petrarch substituted reconstituted
one-size-fits-all   that is all

red sky lullaby universal verse
you do say they may then
when their heart is dis-
carded unregarded find

countersign that vatic
prophetic lines align just so
fencerow neat replete with pithy
lists of atavistic verse galore

therefore before you do pop
sloppily that fat pill in
your bored mouth undoubtedly
hostile because there never was

a pain quite like yours where
there must within ruin be
a word bird-like sweet tweet
that rhymes with the one before

letter to K. about rain and hammers

it sounds to me that you have found peace amidst the banging of a hammer and the dust of creating new things. there is much creation in you. your house, garden, and friends do better with your attention. the roof will be a good thing for you to undertake. perhaps there will be a leak after a hard rain. something tells me that if there is it will be a nice reminder of the hard work you put in. i guess i think of leaks in a roof as a single flaw, necessary and mysterious. origins with such things are not so easy to trace but worth looking into.

this last september i began to appreciate such things as leaks. here is that story. we were back in the valley after a long time away. this part you know, but we returned to daily rains and much green. this we were not used to, so much of two things in a place where we become used to brown. there were daily rains and we, one evening when the sky was especially full, decided to go to church. i've told you about the priest who preaches nothing but devil and damnation. this is a God story. the priest had begun. again he was talking about the fiery furnaces of hell, and then it began to rain.

the church with its tin roof sits in a meadow, very green and full this year. beneath this tin roof there is a single, very small, room with a few wooden pews, an altar, some saints and Jesus on the wall, and at the front a priest. it began to rain very hard. i smiled thinking it was angels, thousands of them, running across the tin roof. the drops of rain on the few windows liked the last of the autumn light and the church was filled with sound and that very same light. the priest worked hard to speak above the rain. today the devil or whatever evil we were supposed to fear in this sermon succumbed to the rain. i was happy. then, Karen, it was silent for a few seconds, the sermon and rain ending almost on cue. it is then that the roof betrayed its flaw. very fast dripping at the rear of the church. here is where man shows his own flaws. from the old wooden rafters at the rear of the church, someone had tied an old coffee can with baling wire. this person had not sought out the source of the leak, a narrow slit, a small lightless hole where a nail had failed to do its job. rather, this person placed a coffee can, a tinny metronome to count the cadence of our meditation.

there is much sound in hammers, roofs, rain, and people's thoughts. the flaw is not always necessary, but it is a way to remember sound after the initial work has rested. you mentioned lent. i think you said something of introspection. that is a carpenter's work and a writer's too. it is a good thing that you are both. a sound maker.

sometimes it will take a dripping roof to make a person write. other times it will be a well hammered note from a friend that you haven't heard from in a long time. both are like the rain, proof of things beyond our own tracing, without origins, but in us like a tinny metronomic heartbeat.

peace, be well.

your amigo
a.

road-sign in holy land

i killed the road-sign

she was ghost dancing
just outside of rosebud
her long black hair
tangled in the wind
hips and legs
pounding the copper shadows
into dry clay

i could hear her thin chants
dying in weak echoes
as she cried to be free
from the clean curves of the road

she cried for the western sun
to crouch above it
to fade like dying light
and drown beneath the Paha Sapa

her hair became raven wings
and in her eyes
she longed to ride the shiny back
of a painted blue horse

so i killed the road-sign

and released her
to follow the sun

for the unidentified mexican national who died at 5:00
p.m. somewhere between san luis and manassa   his van
rolling 3¼ times

tonight i will name you Jose Molina
you are a butterfly in a pine tree
the curve of the mountain
the clouds that ring us
the stars above rubbing into them
a beautiful friction

tonight Jose Molina you are all that we deny
the green fields of the gringos as antonito burns
the dry conejos
the broken winged birds who migrate
to their same fence day after day
the ground beneath them
diamond filled with broken glass
el viejo Moeller saying
"while they drink wine i drink their water"

Jose Molina who came to this country
one of fifty-five lying flat
shoulder to shoulder beneath the false floor of a semi
eighteen hours from vera cruz
where he was baptized in a pink church
is unidentified in today's paper
so that we might call ourselves spanish
and call him wetback
to make it easier to forget him
it is easier really
to be without hope and spanish
than forgotten and mexican

Jose Molina i have seen you before
your silhouetted body facing east
in the door frame of your trailer on a winter morning
trying to become warm
become american
able to tell yourself that you are not cold
tell yourself that a bird caught in fence
is living and not barely alive
that the well dug ten feet too shallow

is potential rather than a failed dream
the only thing that grows during a drought is irony
six generations ago
my abuelo's abuelo saved the mormons
from a winter that would have killed them
fed them with twenty-two of his own cows
for this he was given a tent

i hesitate to write this as much as
Moeller hesitated to steal land
as much as manassa offered water
to their burning neighbors

i am not a racist
nor am i color blind

that field is green
this one is brown

Jose Molina is a man
not a mexican national

the conejos in her old riverbed is dry
the last of her blood diverted north toward manassa

i am not crying for what my ancestors failed to do
i am learning to shout for what my children will need

i am not spanish more than i am mexican
i have not forgotten Jose Molina or my mother

Jose Molina is not his real name
he died poor and mexican in a time of drought

tonight the stars are rubbing themselves
against a distant wall of clouds
there is friction in the air
an electricity that promises
something loud and memorable

something small and unsaid

i never got to tell you
how a warm orange
peeled by your mother
placed on a small white plate
and later in your mouth
will taste sweet as autumn
the earth's ripest hour
your mother's favorite season

a dream of david

day breaks silently on the llano
a thin strip appearing above the san juans
growing wider spreads as it consumes the sky
bringing the dew with it cold and thin
clinging to blades of grass
there are no birds and few rabbits to disturb the silence
it is nothing like the ruckus of sunset

david sits half reclined on an old plastic bucket
that he has nailed a piece of plywood to in order to make it more comfortable
i can tell he is singing
head cocked back tilting to my left
his face pointing east like the breeze
he drinks straight from the bottle
tiny sips that take a long time
draining the bottle very slowly
the tequila is smooth with the soft bite of numbness

i can see the dust swirling like a stampeded procession down the dirt road
david says it looks like a slick
making methodical circles over a dust-off
but i know it is my father coming to relieve me
i have worked all night making my own circles with the tractor and the baler
listening to the incessant thump of the baler
until i became sleepy and began to see brujas
just beyond the razor swath of the headlights
which carved the darkness like a shield protecting me within their thin arms
i imagined i would have seen more had there been no light

i would have seen the brujas making their way
shadows jumping from sage to sage haunting him
replaying all those dead eyes glazed smooth
i would have seen rifle smoke blue like dawn
thin and jumpy like the light in david's square house
a kerosene lamp consuming itself slowly

so when i see david drink himself to sleep
on the edge of the ditch
when he is supposed to be irrigating his beans and potatoes
i understand that maybe he is dreaming
fighting off the dead eyes
i know that the water will creep over the rows of the garden
and congregate in thin streams
making its way to the dirt road
and when he wakes
his small yard and the narrow road will be mud
in a few days all that had been fresh green
will turn and fade to a weak yellow
desperately needing the sun

a letter to Sanchez from antonito while also remembering

Marcos, que tal amigo

here there is something like happiness
and often it is real, the waking at 5:00 a.m. to still see
our moon full in her western sky
i have my llano and my antonito
they are mostly kind and i will treat them as such
yet there is this part of me
a far off part of me that longs for longing
to be far away makes everything seem so much more romantic
and then if not for the moon this morning
i might think that things are in fact very sad
there is no great news from this high windy place
except that i am glad to hear from you
to know that Jessica is someone's angel
and that her wings will push that someone away
in the natural order of things
because even angels come from someplace
and we can't always follow

you and Kathy are good together
have always been
and for the past   she is rarely too good to anyone
love Kathy in your memory and in your future
the past sometimes synonymous with memory
is selective   don't let her select the part of you
that can't forget
let the past be the part of you that chooses
to remember

other than the baby's first breath
memory is the only thing we humans
are capable of making perfect

the rest
the thick maned horses in a winter field
the flowers that will take the horse's place
the river that will give birth to the flower
the mountain that envies

her colorful skirt of towns people and flowers
even as they look up toward her for their inspiration
all that
the rest that is love beyond perfect
is the work of something higher
precious angels perhaps
maybe your father's God
or the poet's eyes

regardless they are beautiful without us
and because of us

so now i'm rambling in some philosophical place
i don't really know how to get out of
but i guess i'm saying that i miss the same things you do
and my desk is older than me
the kids mostly don't care about the poem
they only love the alphabet   the words a - f
and then all of a sudden there is one
a woman in the back of your class
who never says a word
until one day you are talking about language
asking the alphabet lovers how many languages they have
and the conversation leaves english and spanish
moves on two feet toward music   sign language   and dance
and that one woman in the back
she barely raises her hand
and i call on her
"Derika what is your other language"
she waits with her answer as if it were the question
"listening" she says
then my eyes drop because i have been taught
a new language   something born in silence

Marcos Sanchez   listen
find your love in what she tells you
and in what she does not
those people on the phone
the halls of eddy
they sometimes have something to say
but mostly they just talk
and the world does not grow from it
you make the world grow
because you have a woman and daughter that love you
and because you can see through water and time
listen to what the women and water say
if you pay attention
they might be as perfect as memory

much peace from this high place

your bro
a.

an open letter to my creative writing class

dear minion

daily there is a notice of some sort
some mention of the long summer ahead
as our earth waits   dry
for some love

there it is
that word we always wrap ourselves around
the note on the keyboard
we return to
in order to tune ourselves
something in me likes the minor keys
their diminished pulse
that feels like distance
i move daily toward some sad key
perhaps an image of my town
wrapped in dust
my abuelito who only wore
his new teeth once for his funeral
toward my wife
who lives for music
in a valley known for its silence

i guess what i'm saying
is that we all move toward those things
that try and become
because and despite of us

perhaps this is what i mean
Amanda has twice
tried to make this man smile
she asks him
from the deep "heart of an easter lily"
to love something
and he will not
but that is the electricity of the word
for that one seated man
our mind
if only for a few minutes
exists solely to make him smile

sometimes the work of the poem
cannot be realized
we hide it from ourselves
binding what we love
so that it does not venture
into the oncoming lights of pre-dark

i know a brilliant man
born with sight in only one eye
his right eye knowing
what the left can only imagine
in his half blindness
he calls himself left eyed
because that is the place
the poems come from
my friend   John
left eyed   imagines his son back to life
unstalls his son's car
moves it from the side of the road
in the pre-dark of what will
become the rest of John's life
he wills his son
from the deep blue of his left eye
not to get out of the car and begin walking

his poem will never finish
because he wishes
in the paradox of his heart
that poems were not necessary

they are as necessary as pain
necessary as the piano
dormant in the living room
waiting for the hands of an eight year old girl
to hammer out la marcha by ear

weekly i enter your lives
and cast some doubt in your direction
weekly i wonder my confusion
into words and steer my green pen
toward what must be
something like your child stepping from the car
daring to walk toward the oncoming lights

recently i heard that i try
and make everyone write like me
all of you
must know how unfortunate this would be
truth   i suppose i would be happiest
if there was just the one me writing

i want each of you
to find your key on the piano
perhaps sometimes
our voices will harmonize
within the notes of our songs
but know that two voices
will always sound
like two voices

both eyes do not
always see the same thing
D.H. there is no need to apologize for rhyming
it's all good
all push
press
pass and
pray
in the end
that maybe we can all add
poem
to your race alliteration
and surrender ourselves
honestly and completely
as though it were something like movement
something like the harmony
of breathing and moving fast
each gesture
a true word
each word the intonation
of many voices
the rain the paper and all of us pray for

be well adios
a.

zoot suit, a poetic history
much admiration to Luis Valdez

for me the first time i saw a zoot suit
it was like my burning bush
the laws of my culture being passed down
to some punk who did not know his own voice identity people
admittedly i came from a ranching family
speaking spanish wearing levi's
weaned on the stories of men and women
who lived long before my time
these people in the stories
were always like me
from my brown town, with my brown features
other than the brown
i was miles and miles from zoot suits and
calo the beautiful dialect of the urban chicano warrior

despite the miles
i knew that the pachuco
with his reet pleat tacuche and calcos
looking sharp as a diamond was the voice calling to me
it hummed the word remember
in the high valley breeze that surrounded my home

the zoot suit with all its connotations
of chicanismo rebellion affection and later
with its bruises of racism marginalization and assimilation
became the symbol that many wait an entire life to see
the zoot suit was the unwritten history of a beautiful people
estranged in their own land
by too many people who thought they were anything but beautiful

pues an analogy might do to explain my point
you are surrounded by your family su tierra su cultura
everything is as its been for centuries
the towns you live in bear the names of your beautiful language
the dances you attend on saturday night
are full of the powerful notes that is your music
in short you and your life are beautiful
then there is this war
which you did not ask for nor understand

and those things that make you the person you know and understand
are gone forever in the ink of a treaty
whose promise is as empty as the house no one lives in anymore
your language and music while alive become less prominent
you are beaten at your school
because you spoke the language
that flows like the sweet sweet of candy just as you swallow
this is all fact   we all know   things get lost
sometimes forever

ah but the zoot suit saved me
it saved many
the ones people called "dirty mexicans"
wore their zoot suits like warriors in full dress
the ensemble shouted

"*aqui estoy pues i never left*
i am the proud chicano
displaced the to the urban zones
of my former world
and i am rebuilding
aqui estoy mirame beautiful like i've always been"

you see the zoot suit was
in a way our renaissance
our new bandera that said
"*i get it*
i know
i am
i shall always be"

the suit
as is the case with anything fiery
held the curiosity of a nation
and later when the fire of that burning bush said
"*watcha ese*"
it became something to fear
the fear was not homogenized
like some smooth creamy leche
no this fear was brown too

the power structure said
the pachucos were uppity greasers
looking to move in on some turf
reserved for the more privileged
and the brown fear said
look at what we might lose again

but the pachuco prevailed
he stood stonelike
an aztec god in a christian world
and shouted
"orale pues did you think i would leave"
he stood tall
because this warrior represented a proud race
not the hoodlum in the streets the paper claimed was waiting to steal
your purse
no these batos worked hard all day in their jale
wherever that might be
and they came home tired
and sometimes beaten down
by the dust of a job that was their pay
but they came home and found their zoot suit in the closet
glowing like hot coals in the fire
that would be their transformation
and with that transformation
came the pride their beautiful reward
that last look in the mirror
before you head out the door
looking "puro richochet" orale

so you see gente
this is where we leave off
our journey begins
where a centuries old journey
catches its breath
before walking out into the long night
that is the journey of people everywhere
that self-affirming journey that says

"mira aqui estoy
you had me for a while ese
thinking that i was invisible
but look at me gleam
look at my tacuche mi tando y mis tramos
pues yo estoy
how can i say it more clearly
pues i am alive
and i am your memory and your future
let's step out outside and take that walk together
to that place where the music beats like a new heart
where the swing is contagious
and the rucas like being cheek to cheek
follow me batos
to the future
where rhythms blend and the beat is real
pues be careful though
all this dancing and harmony might be catching
pues who would've believed that 60 years ago

vamanos al danzon"

el cerco de prediccion

marks where it all begins
pasando el rio grande
in your mind
y todo esos buen puntadas
about knowing the tattoo
of a man's blood
and why it makes his skin
brown

i will tell you
sometimes the wire
gleams like teeth
hungry

like all those tough skinned
chucos
standing
ay te watcho bold on the corners
of your fear

predictable
the right on vibes
handed out by the hoot suit lengon
preaching right as rain
reforms
so the chicanito/as
can fit the mold
for life on the green side

tearing down
the fence is predictable
it is how we survive
and what we know

so when we come
knocking
at your picket gate
maybe call it a drive-by
ringing of the doorbell

orale
that's just the alarm going off
time to wake up
and realize
that the fence is down
predictably
we're still here

new teeth

it is february
all i can think about
are my abuelito's new teeth
how my father would help him
into the car
before driving to the clinica
where he would sit
boca arriba
still managing to flirt
with the hygenist

what i said earlier
a lie
if only it were the teeth
returning to memory
there is more
a knowing perhaps
that you only wore
those teeth once
knowing the impossibility
that you could make
every woman smile

there is this balancing act
between the sun's weight
and february's cold
between loving and remembering
between a long shadow
growing across a page
and the haunting
that such growth inspires
i loved you
but could not smile at you

you come out of the sun
i feel your shadow grow
across my eight year old body
i am bent over a culvert
looking for baby rabbits
i only remember that i cried

when you finally
let go of my neck
that i failed
to be strong
that i thought you too slow
and that you caught me
without me even moving
i only remember the balance
of the august sun
and your shadow falling across my body

with men
between our loving
and our standing up straight
we can't be understood
my abuelito loved me
he said i wasn't worth a shit
i loved him back
we rarely smiled

later
after you no longer recognized me
i would arrange for you
to get new teeth
your body so much thinner now
that your old ones
no longer fit

i am proud
have always been
the way the lady
took off her glasses
so you could admire the frames
only so you could correct yourself
a butterfly in mid flight
acknowledging that it wasn't
the glasses but her eyes

the new teeth are a symbol
you got them too late
by then you had
stopped eating
having already told us
that they were coming for you
ya vienen por mi
dos hombres y una mujer
it seems cliché or confusing
you told us
you were going home
even as you lay there
in your own living room

i'm still wondering
who the two men were
and that woman
she must've been quite happy
when they arrived
you saying something
much more profound than hello
both of you smiling
everything fresh and final
as new teeth

perhaps tonight we will finally rest

Miguel cannot keep the guitar in tune
one string only
keeps falling
backward into the dissonant night
'too much tension' he finally says
so he loosens
the fourth string
lets the guitar's neck rest
lets the guitar
her one small hand
rest loosely on her body
that way sleep
is easier on all of us

poem for the monsoon

the gray wing
of the silver plane cuts through the dull clouds
descending toward tucson
where later the rain and falling sun
will leave the mountains dressed in blood and orange

already i'm in love with the desert
the nopal thick with their red fruit
saguaros bending their arms into the sun
i drive further into the desert
toward ajo and later mexico
i don't tell anyone that i'm counting roadside crosses
i don't mention that between tucson and the border
there are 104 of them not counting
the number the rest of the desert holds

i only speak when i know the name of something
ocotillo   cholla   agave
already i love the desert
though the road that heaves southward through
desert washes warns me
"do not enter when flooded"
the road heaves southward through mesquite
and the warm mud of the desert monsoon

all of my life i've seen the vans
but here the pale green migra vans are
part of the desert
everywhere there are vans and towers which
look southward across the desert where
last year 135 blistered bodies
never made it to this road

everything in nature seems to move this way
south then north then south a cycle
until finally we accept it
protect it like fenced in sandhill cranes
on a pond reflecting mountains
or butterflies pressed
delicately against a june window

yesterday   a tuesday
i watched a flock of small blackbirds
move south in an october afternoon
from where i stood
their scatter looked round in flight
contracting   expanding
their body fluctuating as if
attached to a shared heart

i try not to think of the blistered bodies
i try not to think of
Wilmer Romero   Angel Sandiero or
Alma Belinda Cruz
i try not to
but i keep seeing the man with the yellow backpack
i keep seeing him
kneeling roadside with 20 others just like him
i keep seeing the two officers with their m-16s
i keep
seeing that damn yellow backpack
the brightest color in all the monsoon

later   because i deal in connections
because my job   the poem says i must
i try and bring that yellow backpack
those 20 men roadside   the 135 dead this year
i try and bring them together with an elk
a cow elk dead at 12,000 feet
her body lying on a treeless ridge in a
meadow of alpine grass
her body caught still by death
her sleek lines still running
uphill toward nothing but more
meadow and that uphill line
where the short grass meets the tall sky

her body is beautiful
there are four of us on the trail
i am the only one to notice her
the only one who finds
her lightning struck body beautiful

if it weren't for the coyotes
who have eaten away at her belly
exposing the bones and flesh
burned from the inside out
if it weren't for the perfect black ring
or burnt grass around her beautiful body
if it were not for the
soft rain that must have
fallen on her newly dead body   thus
putting the fire out
if it weren't for all of this
and that yellow backpack
had i found her in that soft monsoon rain
i would have guessed that
she died of her own motion
that her sleek body
propelled forward   legs extended
nose pointing toward the tall sky
i would have guessed that beauty
or the small calf undoubtedly running beside her
all of that   all of this heaviness in the thin air
all of this   the motion of her long legs
the scattering of the herd around her
perhaps the monsoon killed her
there is more than one way to burn
water cannot always save us
often it barely eases what is burning

this year's monsoon will not leave me
the grain in my father's field
swells with each day's gift
each body swells with the day's passing
each day swells with the memory
of the desert in bloom
each day swells with the memory of 20 men
and one yellow backpack
each day the sun swells its body
and throws light on a shrine to la virgen in sasabe mexico
sun escapes from la virgen's body
she rests on a moon
an angel holds up the moon
here is where people   before the desert
pray

they are people   their hearts pump
like a flock of south flying blackbirds
this shrine is where people pray
for their crossing to be safe
these people pray
and if nature has an equivalent
it must be something blooming or
a cow elk caught running toward
a high meadow's edge or
grain swelling with daily rain or
Jose Angel Hernandez eating a mango
though he will never see his son again

perhaps prayer is yellow
perhaps the prayer
we all everyone everything carries in migration
is small enough to fit in a backpack
a yellow backpack in a blooming desert
perhaps a prayer   if left to its own voice
will flutter in its yellow cage
rest against the window that is the border
and someday fly through
moving beautifully toward that line where
prayer ends   desert blooms   sky descends
and monsoon begins

san acacio garage an update

they tore her down

i thought that garage
blooming from the llano
like those cactus my abuelita liked so much
would last forever

joe's ethereal garage
specializing in holly carbs
four bolt mains
domed pistons
and cruising machines
which roll south
through the town of san acacio
the worlds greatest detox center
eight miles in one direction
32 in another and too many
in the other two
from a drop of wine

damn that town aint seen grapes
since 1932 when ms. san acacio
used em as a prop in her fruit of love skit
man was that a sweet sweet chingon scene
when she started feeding them to herself
b/c juan the king of atzlan and leading man
had a rally to attend

the garage been
down down
for awhile now
ay ay ay ay
recycle those adobes bro
just in case
you know
that fool comes back from the dead
driving that trans am that went off the road
in '82 looking for the carb he meant to pick up
but couldn't because
doña SSSSS
insisted he didn't need no four barrels
where he was going

what was that cat's name
just know he drove that sweet sweet chingon
trans am   the color of ms. san acacio's eyes

when i asked him how beautiful he answered in metaphor

called her a lake
he saw when he was eight
blue like depth
can only make blue

called her roads blowing
into and away
from one another
spoke of shadows and their lines
the unchasable tail
madrugada

afterward he cursed the timing of things
said things like
the winter was too long
or if only summer
would have been
a bit greener

he answered with mountains
said he would want to go there again
past the gold camps at 12,000 feet
over the aspen fingers december bare
following the river
lined with black birds perched
on icy edges
up the canyon
to the lake he saw
when he was eight
so beautiful
that eighty years later
he went there
before heaven

he told me
the earth's skin
was brown that morning
like women
braiding their hair
in dimly lit kitchens

he loved the color blue
how the trees followed
the river like school kids

he loved her like miles of time
he loved her like stones
thrown into a river
his love could scare the fish away

her eyes that morning
were dark and golden
all at once
the lake was blue
as though God on this day
loved water more than sky

a letter to Pablo about hope

And one morning it was all ablaze,
and one morning firestorms
erupted from the earth
and from then on, flames,
and in the streets the blood of children
flowed simply, like blood from children.

                    - Pablo Neruda

this earth
whose rain and locomotive whistles you loved
is burning   once again
and in the streets
they mostly show women with pictures
who look upward
and that is why i call this letter hope

do you already know
was it the birds
who under their wings
bring autumn from the north
one cold morning at a time
or was it the smoke
filled with gray screams
of a history that repeats itself

right now i am wondering
which sign i should follow
i could not find paper
but there was that other voice
which pointed to this piece of cardboard
Pablo   there must be poets everywhere
trying to explain a few things
and now we know why simile fails
when she is dressed in flames
here it has rained during the night
and in new york

it is also raining and a friend says
even the birds have stopped
here the sky is calm
and the birds line themselves
on the fences   notes of music
in the early fog of the cooling earth
they begin again
and still i cannot explain the streets
and i suppose i know why
the birds have given up their singing

Pablo   tell me
is there an image
that word capable a gesture for flames
and another for people who hope
because in the streets
people wait like people waiting
and perhaps they wish their pictures
were not of suits dresses and smiles
but of some deep earth of ash
so we might really know
from the paper taped to the bus stop vestibule
who is sleeping and who is sleeping
beyond the last shrinking days of summer

here is a truth   i am afraid
the wound will remind itself of its origins

did the earth
has the earth
will it ever forgive itself
for its fire
Pablo
i am here with my pen
i wish it were green
it is the color of the sky before a storm
so i write to you knowing
that a poem with its
heartbeat of syllables
can change nothing

yet words keep on
simply like words that must keep on
in them   too   there is hope
that looks up towards things
and the word   on two feet
tries to build again
even when no one listens

dear Pablo
your birthplace of oceans
is trying to forgive itself
as the men work in the rain
and 2000 miles away i am writing
on the back of a piece of cardboard
hoping
that anything dressed in anger
will not repeat itself
i know it will
and that is why in the streets
the poets must at least try
we must at the very least
remind the sky
that there is something like prayer
in the smoke
and that soon enough
the birds will begin again

Printed in the United States
72364LV00004B/179